Get ready, you guys. It's time

ADVENTURES
in
DRAWING
A Guided Sketchbook
by Scott C.
and

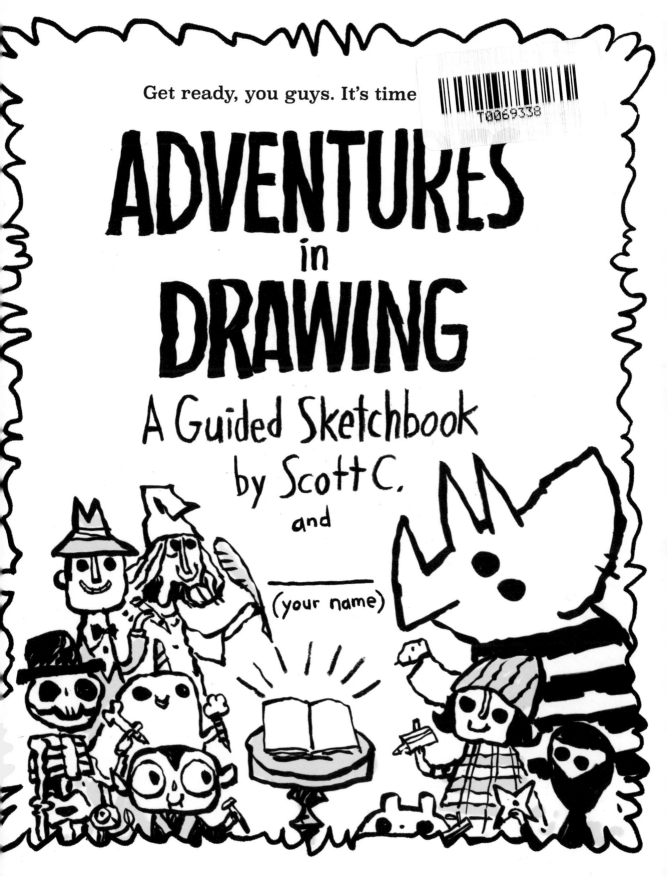

_____
(your name)

INSIGHT 👁 EDITIONS
San Rafael, California

Hello, there! Welcome to this drawing book! I am Scott C., your guide and sidekick as we journey deep into this incredible world together, creating it as we go. Get ready to tap into your deep-down imaginative brains.

This is me!

I often draw myself like this because it is what I look like in real life, but I can draw myself any way I want to. As artists, we can change ourselves into anything, just like magicians!

Here I am as . . .

a tree!

a walking cube!

a round ball!

an alligator!

a doggie!

an ant!

For this book, I have decided to draw myself as a bunny. Bunnies are very cozy creatures. Let's get cozy and have fun with our brains!

In fact, that is the entire purpose of this book. Let your mind go! Don't think too much. Don't put so much pressure on your poor brains. Allow them to just flow down imagination river.

One way we can take the pressure off our brains is to draw lots and lots of versions of the same thing. That way none of the drawings really need to be that great, and your brains will be able to relaaaax.

Let's try drawing a bunch of versions of *you*. The crazier we get, the better the ideas become! I will suggest some versions for you to try right now:

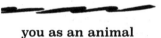

you normally

you as a food

you as a triangle

you as an animal

you as a star

you as a cloud

you as a poppyseed

Haha, those are wonderful! Man, you nailed yourself. Right on.

If you let your clever brains just do their thing, I'll bet they'll surprise you with what they can come up with! You will be swimming in a sea of wild ideas!

Wheels! Pies! Snakes with hats! Sometimes we all get a little stuck with ideas and need some brain joggling. That's completely normal. I'll pop in every once in a while and suggest things for you to draw. I will call this the **IDEA ZONE**!

What do we draw with? This book is about enjoying yourself, so use whatever you want. Try switching things up! Sometimes that feels good. Get those colors out if that sounds fun. Here are just a few things you might want to try using:

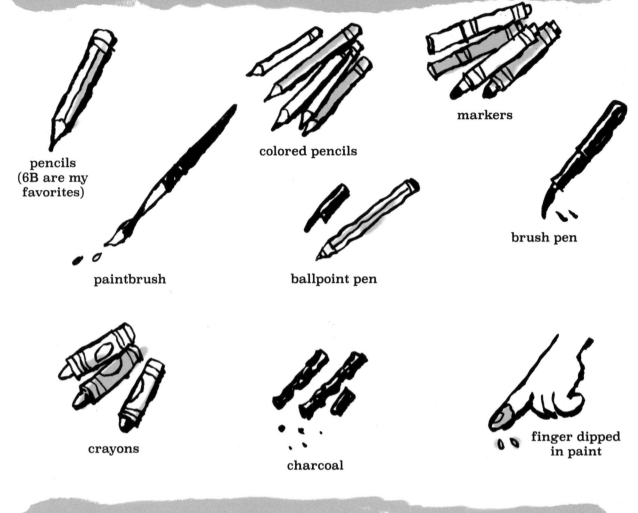

pencils
(6B are my
favorites)

colored pencils

markers

paintbrush

ballpoint pen

brush pen

crayons

charcoal

finger dipped
in paint

Where do we draw? Let's get comfortable! What are some pleasant spots to relax our minds? Let me throw some ideas out for you . . .

table with chair

bench

couch

ground

tree stump

Let's get our brains loose! I will suggest some things for you draw right now. Draw them quick, but have fun.

a worm!

a rock!   a flower!

a sun!

a hat!   a leaf!

Now try putting faces on them!

By the way, if you ever run out of space and want to keep riffing on any ideas, just grab some more scratch paper and keep drawing. You can just stuff those pages into this book for safe keeping.

Do you like coloring? Well, go nuts! Color anything you want in this book, including me sitting on this rock!

What about erasers? There are no mistakes in this book! Only fun experiments. So if something doesn't look like you wanted, turn it into something new or draw something else, but try to not use erasers!

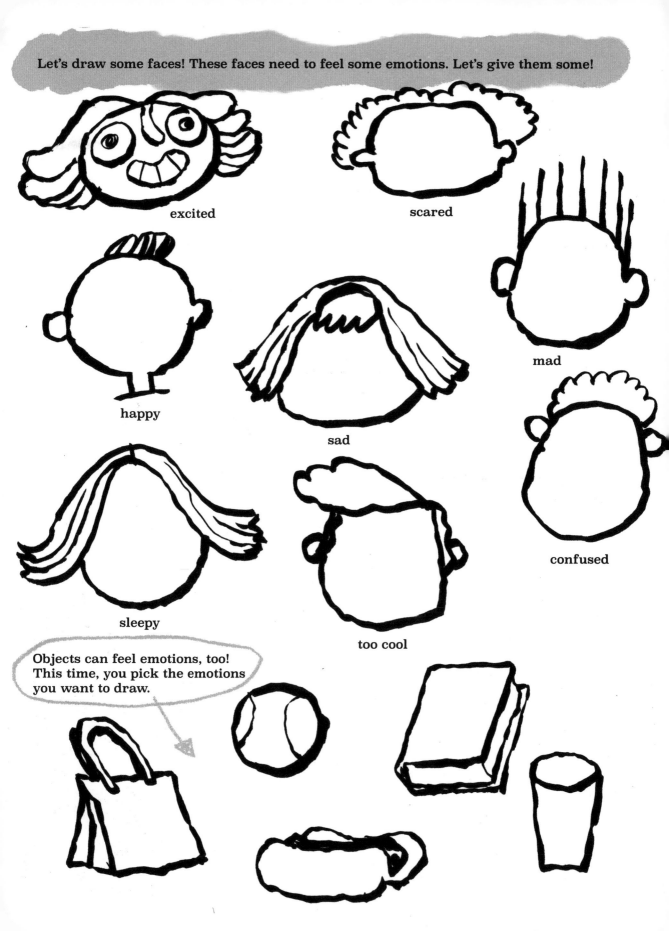

Let's draw some faces! These faces need to feel some emotions. Let's give them some!

excited

scared

mad

happy

sad

confused

sleepy

too cool

Objects can feel emotions, too! This time, you pick the emotions you want to draw.

The list exercise! I love making lists before I start drawing to help my brain loosen up. Want to try it? I'll say a word, and you just write things the word reminds you of. Could be absolutely anything. They don't even have to relate to the original word! This is just to get your mind thinking and working properly! It is sometimes called free writing or brainstorming. No wrong answers here!

The word is . . . *tree.*

BIRD!

_____   _____

_____   _____

_____   _____

_____   _____

_____   _____

_____   _____

_____   _____

_____   _____

Look at all these wild ideas. Now let's draw! Fill up the space below with little drawings inspired by the things you wrote above.

We are about to embark on our drawing journey here, so let's do just a few more warm-ups! I am going to write another word, and then you *draw* all the things that word makes you think of. Are you ready? Here we go. The word is . . . BALL.

(Here are some of the things I think of.)

You can do this exercise starting with a picture as well! Let me draw something for you here. Use this drawing as a starting point, and see what you come up with!

IDEA ZONE: A heavy shoe! A bubble shoe! A sad shoe! A rain shoe! A toy! A sandcastle! A bird! A crab with a cool hat! An odd car! A vase with flowers!

Characters! We will meet all kinds of characters in this book that we will draw together. Let's try creating a character right now! We can use all the brainstorming exercises we have learned so far. Let me suggest a character for you to draw:

Meet Sneaky Mouse! This mouse is very good at hiding and sneaking around like a spy. The mouse loves gadgets and things that help him be sneaky. This mouse can be wearing whatever you want, or nothing at all!

List random stuff here:

Draw things inspired by your list here:

⬇

Now draw some sneaky mice here! Combine your list and doodles into characters. Circle your favorite design, and give your mouse a name!

I love this mouse!

Where does this mouse live? List a wild variety of house ideas, and start going crazy! I've drawn some outlines already.

Brainstorm list:

_____

_____

_____

_____

_____

_____

_____

_____

_____

_____

_____

_____

_____

shoe house

mushroom house

tin can house

_____ house

_____ house

_____ house

I would visit any of those wonderful houses!
Haha. I feel pretty warmed up. How about you?
I think we are ready for our journey to begin.

Here we go! We are off to meet some interesting people and see some delightful things in town. Help me populate this place! Add the following things to this picture anywhere you like: A bird! A person with a cake! A worm! A dog! A plane! A cloud! A blimp! A car! A flower! A bug! Some store signs! A mailbox! A burglar! A manhole with an alligator peeking out! A bear! Someone singing! Someone playing a horn! And add some townspeople in the windows!

Look at all these local townspeople strolling about with glorious hats on their heads. Let's help them out. Draw some crazy, grand, magnificent hats on their heads so we can all enjoy them together.

These townspeople are out walking their pets! What do their pets look like? I want to know if they are dangerous-looking or friendly because I will behave a certain way depending on what you draw . . .

a flower pet?

a puffy pet?

a slippery pet?

IDEA ZONE: Pets can be anything! Dogs, cats, alligators, beetles, monsters, tubas, robots, dragons—so many options!

Ah, I love this spot! It's the enchanted garden. What peculiar things grow in this delightful place? Plants? Flowers? Berries? Tulips? Let's fill it up with things!

It's the town market! Everyone has set up little seller stands trying to sell us their favorite things. Why don't you draw stuff for them to sell so they can attract some solid business?

Psst! **IDEA ZONE:** Each seller has distinct interests. There could be ninja stuff, pirate stuff, stuff cats might like, or hats for the gentlemen and gentleladies!

Bartholomew the inventor of useful and useless things has come to show off his latest inventions. Well . . . he has the names figured out at least. Perhaps you could draw his inventions for him!

bubble car

pumpkin lamp

fuzzy chair

ice cream sled

snake car

kite castle

(you name one!)

flying boot

It's the shoe shop! These poor shoes are without people. Put some people or animals or anything into these shoes so they may walk out into town and have some adventures!

Interior design time! Tabitha has invited us to help furnish and decorate her apartment. She loves music, horses, and cupcakes, so anything inspired by those things would make her really happy.

IDEA ZONE: This room could use things like a dinner table, couch, television, rugs, wall hangings, desk, books, and shelves. And what about making versions of these things inspired by cupcakes, horses, and music?

Hey, you! Take a break and design my shirt. I love mountains, trees, stripes, and beach time!
Oh, this is my buddy Ronald. He's a good guy. He'll love whatever you draw.

Can you please help me paint the library? I do not know what colors would look good on this thing! I'll bet you have some ideas. You can add anything you want to make it more fun, like slides, polka dots, or stripes. Be quiet though! Everyone is reading in there.

IDEA ZONE: Add some people inside the library reading! A pet or two! Some flags! Flowers or nice plants!

The astronomers have launched their science capsule deep into the far reaches of space! What do they see out there? Planets and comets? Aliens and UFOs? Satellites and rocket ships? Draw your version of outer space so the astronomers can get excited and take down some space notes. And perhaps we can journey even farther into the unknown . . .

IDEA ZONE: What if there were space animals out here like monkeys, elephants, and chipmunks? Or star cars, or asteroids made of cheese and bread? I mean, you could put anything out there floating around. A cup of freshly brewed space tea would be nice.

We have definitely reached a magical place: the Land of Magic and Wonder. Who have we found up here living with the candy bees, unicorns, and cloud heads? Draw some creatures we have never seen before!

IDEA ZONE: Flying creatures! Puffy planes and blimps! Rainbow creatures! Angels! A flying ant! A whale with wings!

Oh my goodness! Unicorns live in this magical place! Unicorns are shy creatures, so only their horns are visible. Why don't you draw some unicorns to go with those horns and coax them out of their shy zones?

A

A

Can I have a horn, too?

IDEA ZONE: Unicorns can be anything
you want! They can be dogs or bears or
worms or cars, basketballs or ghosts or
even just a box with a horn on it!

It's dance party time in the Land of Magic and Wonder! Puff Head has started the dance floor. Draw the other dancers and their amazing dance poses. I added a few things to help get you started.

a round person

a fluffy person

a teeny person

IDEA ZONE: All kinds of animals and creatures have been invited. Peacocks, bears, rabbits, fish, cows, termites, bugs, montsters, rainclouds, unicorns, flying squirrels!

a spikey person

a very skinny person

Oh, boy, I smell some *sweets*. I'd love to enjoy some strange sweets. Let's design some! Remember, this is a magical place where candies and desserts can be any shape and size, so color them any way you want. Make them look almost too wonderful to eat!

Excuse me! Can you help me build a cotton candy house, where I will live and invite my friends to play? Thank you so much! I like candy canes, gumdrops, ice cream slides, flags, birds, bubbles, stairs, windows, roof decks, swimming pools, and winged elephants. So feel free to include any of those things, or anything you like. You are the *best*!

Whew! I may have hit my sweet and magical threshold. What do you say we head back to solid ground? I am ready!

Ah, the good old solid ground of the lush countryside. Check out these happy farmers and their charming little homestead. They raise adorable animals on their farm. Let's draw these delightful creatures for them!

Catsie's house!

IDEA ZONE: These weird crops can come in all shapes and sizes. Square shapes, pear shapes, long and skinny, bubbly . . . and they can have all kinds of patterns like stripes, polka dots, plaid, and paisley. And you can even give them some horns, hats, or ties!

Catsie has invited us into her little country house for tea. Why don't we take this opportunity to color her house in? She has lots of baby kittens, so you might also want to draw cats everywhere lazing about. They could be hiding, reading, napping, drinking milk—you decide!

A mystery character has come to have some tea with us! This mysterious character is very wise and loves honey sandwiches. What kinds of creatures can you think of that fit this description?

List your ideas here:

_____

_____

_____

_____

_____

_____

_____

_____

_____

_____

_____

_____

_____

Doodle your ideas here:

Now let's draw some houses for this little fellow. In a stump? Under a rock? In a hole? In a little hut?

I feel like it's time for some hugs. Let's give all these characters someone or something to hug. I am excited to feel the warmth of these hugs.

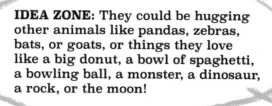

IDEA ZONE: They could be hugging other animals like pandas, zebras, bats, or goats, or things they love like a big donut, a bowl of spaghetti, a bowling ball, a monster, a dinosaur, a rock, or the moon!

Now we are deep in the forest, where the forest creatures are hiding and playing games. Where are they all? Let's find them! Draw some squirrels, bugs, rabbits, deer, bears, and whatever else you think might be hiding around here. Let's fill the forest with hiding creatures!

Oh, wow! Ssshhh. Quiet down a sec. There are some rare deer grazing nearby. These deer have unusual antlers. Why don't you draw them in? I am curious to see what they look like.

IDEA ZONE: Antlers can be any bizarre shape. Try curlicues! Squiggles! Trees! Baseball bats! Rainbows! Radar dishes! Your name in cursive!

Here comes Happy Tree cruising down the forest path! Happy Tree is happiest when her branches are filled with birds. Draw some birds on her branches, and we will see how happy she can get!

Even though these birds live in the forest, they love to hang out in cages in their free time. Let's draw some fancy cages. They could be round or square or squiggly or anything your mind comes up with . . .

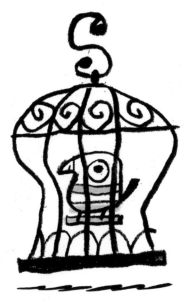

Oh, no! Poor Rhino has eaten something to make her tummy upset. What could she have eaten? Please draw what she ate so we can try to help her.

IDEA ZONE: Could be anything! A big hamburger, a boulder, a band of ninjas, an airplane, a princess, a big tire, a bicycle, some bricks, a house, who knows!

Oh, look! The lumberjacks are crafting logs for the forest creatures to ride around in. Let's populate this little clearing with various smiling or frowning logs and their animal friends!

We've run into a group of bigfoots. But these bigfoots are so cold! Keep them warm by giving them some fur with scribbles and scratches and puffs. If you feel like they need some scarves, then give them scarves!

Oh my goodness, it has really gotten cold around here. We must have entered some sort of arctic landscape. This little fellow looks warm, though. Looks like he is enjoying a bit of ice fishing. Let's draw some crazy underwater fish and other creatures that might be roaming in the icy waters below.

IDEA ZONE: We could also find sunken ships, sea monsters, or killer whales down here.

Polar Bear is having a really hard time concentrating on her book. Her neighbors are so loud! Can you draw her neighbors in the igloo next door so we can see who is making all this racket? Maybe we can tell them to quiet down at some point.

IDEA ZONE: There could be penguins or snow dogs or killer whales or seals living next door. Or even giants or skeleton teens! They could be playing music, watching TV, having a party, or playing a loud game.

The King needs our help in the olden times, it seems! He has a grand castle but no people in it! Let's inhabit it with knights, princesses, squires, wizards, and royal cats. Draw 20 characters all over this castle doing all sorts of royal and unroyal things!

IDEA ZONE: You can draw people scaling the castle, baking, engaging in swordplay, playing music, exercising, painting portraits, enjoying some castle toys—and you can make kid knights, princess knights, monster knights, whatever you want!

Flags! Now that it is truly a flourishing castle, let's draw some flags. Draw some interesting flags that might be flying over these castle towers.

There are some fine-looking royal animals riding through the castle grounds. Can you draw some knights and princesses riding these glorious animals?

This right here is the highest room in the highest tower. It is where the wizards work on their spells and potions. Let's fill it with wizard things!

IDEA ZONE: Add spellbooks, potions, scrolls, wizard posters, wizard games, wizard spiders, wizard pizza, rugs, baby dragons, or other magically enhanced animals.

A fearless knight has been sent into the rough lands to rid the kingdom of some vicious *dragons*! They live up in that cave, but they have burst forth to greet the brave knight. Draw them all in so the knight knows what he is battling. I see some dragon parts, but not all of them.

Dragon's cave

Wonderful job! Let's leave the knight to his dragons and venture further back into historical times. I am talking waaaaaay back. I know of some creatures that I think you will be very happy to meet.

Dinosaurs! I knew you would like to see these magnificent creatures. Welcome to the age of dinosaurs and volcanoes, where there are even some cavepeople strolling about. Why don't you bestow some colors upon this ancient scene? Add some dinosaurs and cavepeople of your own while you're at it!

IDEA ZONE: What if the dinosaurs had outfits, hats, and boots? That would be crazy. Cavepeople might have wild prehistoric tools.

These dinosaurs are terrified. The biggest, most incredible dinosaur ever beheld by animal eyes has just stepped onto the page. Draw this wonderous beast!

We all love dinosaurs, even down in Monsterland! Kid Vampirello is playing with his dinosaur toys in the vampire family room. What does the decor of this vampire family room look like? Are vampire books and toys lying about? And what about any other vampire family members? Vampire pets?

IDEA ZONE: Think about what might be in a family room . . . a fireplace, a couch, some lamps, paintings, a piano . . . Now combine that stuff with what vampires might like! Candles, coffins, bats, blood, moons . . .

We might as well visit Dr. Franklin's lab while we are here in Monsterland. Whoa! Dr. Franklin! What has happened? You have been messing around with your monster-creating equipment again. What wild monsters have you created this time?

I am sorry! I was just having some monster-lab fun with some new animal brains. I did not realize my experiments would create these *monsterosities!*

snake ghost

flower ghost

hat ghost

Agh! Good work. Now let's get out of here!

It's zombie picnic time! Now this is more like it. I love a good zombie picnic. Help me draw zombies enjoying some zombie games and zombie snacks!

IDEA ZONE: Picnic activities may include horseshoes, kite flying, soccer, softball, croquet, tag, and bug collecting. Try combining this stuff with things zombies like: brains, tombstones, dirt, coffins, missing limbs, and dirty clothes. Maybe they invited some vampire, mummy, and werewolf friends!

Oh my! The old crypt is really happening right now. Looks like a mummy wiggle and jiggle party. Mummies all over the place just wigglin' around. Draw those wild mummies!

Give me some wrappings, please, so that I may wiggle and jiggle.

IDEA ZONE: Anything can be a mummy! Dogs, monkeys, turtles, fish, giraffes. And what about objects like kites, boom boxes, tea sets, and cars? Just wrap them!

This skeleton family is in need of some clothes. They are freezing! Some need pants, some need shirts, some need dresses and blouses, some need hats and shoes. Help them out please, so they can go about their skeleton business in peace!

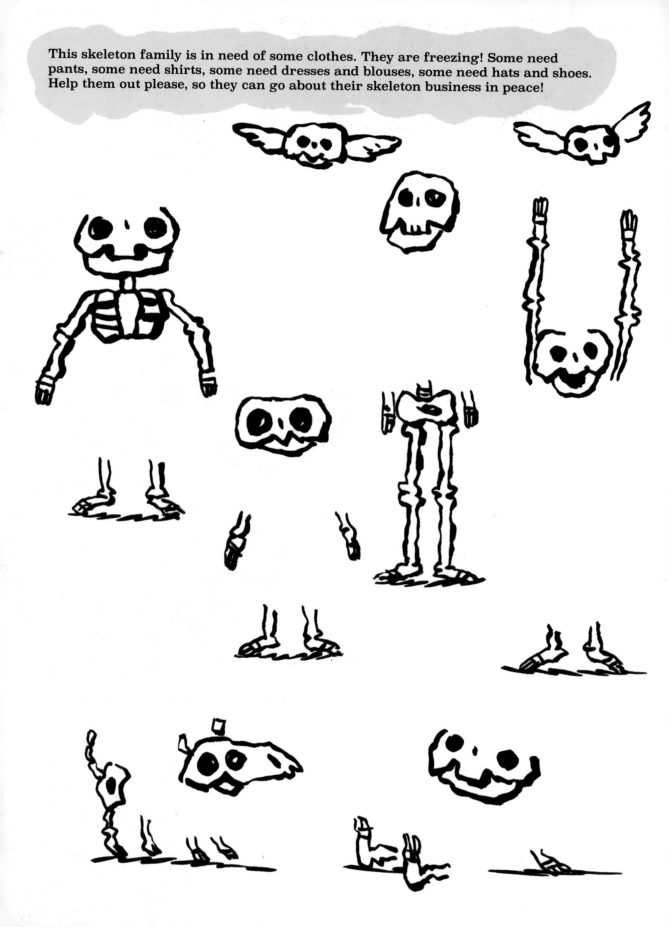

These monster drivers want to do some joyriding! Why don't you give them what they want? Take a look at each driver and think about what each one might love in a car, and then *draw it!*

The mummy car!

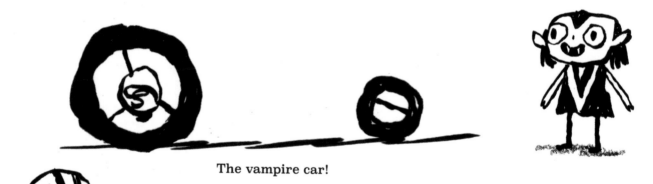

The vampire car!

The skeleton car!

The werewolf car!

The cyclops car!

Little bird wants a car, too.

Mousers already has one.

Let's feed the monsters! The monsters are really hungry and we do not want them to eat us, so let's feed them some food they might like. The grosser the better, I say. You can never be too careful with monsters.

We are nearing the end of the book. Time for some quiet reflection. Let's all relax and spend some time with our thoughts. What is everyone thinking about during this peaceful time?

Let us leave this world in style and give the characters in this book a great time. We have met so many wonderful townsfolk, unicorns, dinosaurs, knights, princesses, monsters, and animals. Populate this splendid scene with partying and playing!

Oh my gosh, I had so much fun drawing with you! Thank you for creating this place with me. I told you your brains would impress you. I was sure impressed! I hope you keep creating worlds. And until we meet again . . . I am going to enjoy this page of stuff you draw for me. So long!

Oh! I forgot to mention one last thing. . . . Remember that you can do these little brainstorm exercises whenever you want with your own sketchbooks and art materials! Start with a word, phrase, place, or thing. Then start riffing on that word by making a list of related thoughts.

Word or words: _____

List of thoughts:

_____ _____

_____ _____

_____ _____

_____ _____

_____ _____

_____ _____

_____ _____

Then draw a bunch of random things inspired by the thoughts you just wrote!

Drawings of things:

Now draw them all together in one wonderful scene!

Haha yay! I love it!

INSIGHT EDITIONS

PO Box 3088
San Rafael, CA 94912
www.insighteditions.com

 Find us on Facebook: www.facebook.com/InsightEditions
 Follow us on Twitter: @insighteditions

Copyright © 2018 by Scott Campbell

All rights reserved. Published by Insight Editions, San Rafael, California, in 2018. No part of this book may be reproduced in any form without written permission from the publisher.

Library of Congress Cataloging-in-Publication Data available.

ISBN: 978-1-68383-121-1

Publisher: Raoul Goff
Associate Publisher: Vanessa Lopez
Art Director: Chrissy Kwasnik
Designer: Amy DeGrote
Senior Editor: Rossella Barry
Associate Managing Editor: Lauren LePera
Editorial Assistant: Maya Alpert
Production Manager: Sadie Crofts

Insight Editions would like to thank Greg Solano for his editorial help.

ROOTS of PEACE   REPLANTED PAPER

Insight Editions, in association with Roots of Peace, will plant two trees for each tree used in the manufacturing of this book. Roots of Peace is an internationally renowned humanitarian organization dedicated to eradicating land mines worldwide and converting war-torn lands into productive farms and wildlife habitats. Roots of Peace will plant two million fruit and nut trees in Afghanistan and provide farmers there with the skills and support necessary for sustainable land use.

Manufactured in China by Insight Editions

10 9 8 7 6 5 4 3 2 1